BEST-LOVED
CHINESE
PROVERBS

Also by Theodora Lau

The Handbook of Chinese Horoscopes

BEST-LOVED
CHINESE
PROVERBS

Theodora Lau

HarperPerennial
A Division of HarperCollinsPublishers

HarperCollins books may be purchased for educational, business, or sales promotional use. For information please write: Special Markets Department, HarperCollins Publishers, Inc., 10 East 53rd Street, New York, NY 10022.

FIRST EDITION

Designed by R. Caitlin Daniels

Library of Congress Cataloging-in-Publication Data
Lau, Theodora.
    Best-loved Chinese proverbs / Theodora Lau.
        p. cm.
    ISBN 0-06-095133-8
    1. Maxims, Chinese. I. Title.
PN6307.C5L38   1995
089'.951—dc20   95-25167

95 96 97 98 99 ❖/RRD 10 9 8 7 6 5 4 3 2 1

Introduction

The appeal of Chinese proverbs has always been profound and universal. The beauty of these statements is in their brevity and simplicity. Their mission to give a direct message that will reach the heart and mind of the reader is often achieved with aplomb and finesse.

These down-to-earth and succinct compositions summarize and crystallize the penetrating wit and wisdom of the Han people for the benefit of all. Like intense beams of light, these proverbs highlight truths in life that are evident but often ignored or unrealized.

The Chinese maxims here were derived indirectly from old Chinese texts. Being interpreted in English not only brings out their timeless value but gives new dimensions in expression. These well-tested truths of condensed knowledge can once again be used to observe and to instruct.

Most of the proverbs here are poetically expressed in the words of the authors. They are original verse, not verbatim translations of any Chinese text. Some are not even translations at all but distillations of several sayings from different sources. Because of the antiquity of these sayings, all have unknown origins. Different regions of China may also have different versions. But, as they say, to truly know a people, know their proverbs.

It is my belief that the value of Chinese proverbs has only increased with the passing of the ages because they ring as true today as they have for thousands of years before.

I have retrieved, molded, and polished these maxims to introduce them in a new and revealing light. I hope you will enjoy reading them as much as I loved writing them for you.

Theodora Lau

A Word About the Chinese Calligraphy by Kenneth Lau in This Book

All the Chinese calligraphy here is in the proper unabbreviated form of original and traditional Chinese, not the simplified version commonly used in China today. This traditional form of calligraphy is followed in Hong Kong, Taiwan, and Singapore and is an important part of Chinese culture.

All the words have auspicious meanings and are meant to be positive, uplifting, or inspiring. Chinese characters denoting negative or inauspicious meanings are generally not exhibited, as their influence is considered unlucky and unhappy for people.

There are about 5,000 Chinese characters or words commonly used in the language; when these are combined, they produce a rich and powerful vocabulary of new words and usage totaling over 100,000. Sometimes a single character will suffice, as in the words *love, endurance, fortune,* and *livelihood,* but in most instances compound characters are used to clarify, emphasize, and deepen the meaning. Compound characters eliminate any possibility of confusion, double meaning, or misinterpretation, for written Chinese is precise in expression.

Chinese is a pictorial language based on drawn symbols rather than sound. Words are classified according to their "radical," or root, and are located under the corresponding class. If one is looking for a word related to water, such as juice, river, stream, or rain, one will find all these words having the common sign of water 水 (radical: 氵) incorporated into their written form. Likewise, emotions will all have the heart 心 radical contained in their written form to describe where the word is derived from.

The pronunciation key given here is based on the modern Chinese phonetic alphabet.

ABILITY	jì	技	skill, trick
	néng	能	energy, ability
ADMIRATION	xiàn	羨	envy, jealousy
	mù	慕	admire, praise
COOPERATION	xié	協	a joint, three symbols of strength 力, combined effort
	zhù	助	help, assistance
COURTESY	lǐ	禮	etiquette, salute, rite, ceremony
	mào	貌	appearance, proper manners
DILIGENCE	qín	勤	hardworking, industrious
	fèn	奮	exert oneself vigorously
FORESIGHT	yuen	遠	far-reaching
	xièn	見	sight, vision

FORTUNE	fú	福	to have wealth, happiness, good prospects, and the ability to enjoy these blessings
HAPPINESS	xǐ	禧	jubilation, joy, felicity, auspiciousness
HONOR	róng	榮	flourish, abundance
	yù	譽	fame, reputation, renown
INSPIRATION	gǔ	鼓	drum up, encourage
	wǔ	舞	dance
KNOWLEDGE	zhī	知	to know, to understand
	shí	識	to recognize
LIVELIHOOD	shēng	生	born, to give birth
	huó	活	daily life, live, livelihood
LONGEVITY	shòu	壽	long life, continuity

LOVE	aì	愛	emotion coming from the center of the heart
MORALITY	daò	道	road, way, path
	dé	德	virtue, ethics
OPPORTUNITY	jī	機	chance, opportunity
	huì	會	ability
PATIENCE	nài	耐	endurance
	xīn	心	of the heart
PERSEVERANCE	rěn	忍	to bear, to endure, to persevere, to have a knife above the heart
PROFIT	lì	利	benefit, advantage
	rùn	潤	flow, lubricate, smooth
SINCERITY	chéng	誠	honest, sincere
	yì	意	intention, idea, meaning

STRATEGY	cè	策	a plan, a scheme
	lüè	略	strategy
SUCCESS	chéng	成	to become accomplished, acquire
	gōng	功	merit, achievement, skill
SUPERIORITY	yōu	優	dominant, preponderance
	shì	勢	position
VICTORY	shèng	勝	success
	lì	利	strength
WEALTH	cái	財	rich, in abundance
	fù	富	wealth, money
WISDOM	zhì	智	wit, wisdom
	huì	慧	bright perception, intelligence

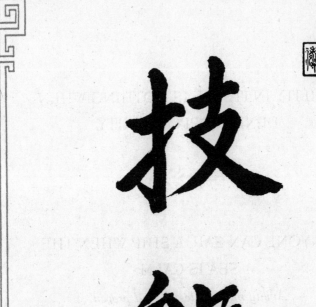

ABILITY

ABILITY IN ITSELF IS NOTHING WHEN
DENIED OPPORTUNITY.

ANYONE CAN SAIL A SHIP WHEN THE
SEA IS CALM.

Ability must be tested and proven.

SOMETHING AS EASY AS BLOWING
OFF DUST.

A very easy task to be done immediately.

CONTROL THE WINDS BY TRIMMING
YOUR SAILS.

LIMITATIONS ARE BUT BOUNDARIES
CREATED INSIDE OUR MINDS.

ONLY TIME AND EFFORT
BRINGS PROFICIENCY.

*There is no shortcut to proficiency without
hard work and applying oneself.*

FIRST ATTAIN SKILL;
CREATIVITY COMES LATER.

A common Chinese adage that means creativity is a natural result of having attained mastery of a task.

CLUMSY BIRDS HAVE NEED OF EARLY FLIGHT.

A common Chinese proverb encouraging those with less ability or with handicaps to work harder instead of making excuses in order to keep up with the rest of the team.

AN OLD BROOM HAS ITS VALUE.

A Chinese proverb stressing the value of previous contacts and warning against discarding old friends or people who have helped you.

MAKE THE CAP FIT THE HEAD.

Know where and when to make adjustments.

BETTER TO BEND IN THE WIND
THAN TO BREAK.

*The flexible bamboo will survive a storm with less
damage than the mighty oak.*

DO NOT BRING KINDLING TO
PUT OUT A FIRE.

Good intentions but wrong solution.

ADMIRATION

ONE WHOSE BREATH IS
FELT IN HEAVEN.

*Denotes a person of great consequence
and importance.*

NO MATTER HOW TALL THE
MOUNTAIN, IT CANNOT BLOCK
OUT THE SUN.

*Common saying of parents who idolize their offspring
and liken the child or the child's abilities to the sun.*

ADVERSITY IS A MIRROR THAT
REVEALS ONE'S TRUE SELF.

UNLESS THERE IS OPPOSING WIND,
A KITE CANNOT RISE.

Opposition and adversity give us a chance
to rise to new heights.

DANGEROUS ENEMIES WILL MEET
AGAIN IN NARROW STREETS.

In life, paths of old foes will often be unexpectedly
crossed again in difficult circumstances.

OUR ENEMIES TEACH US LIFE'S MOST
VALUABLE LESSONS.

TO EAT THE WIND AND SWALLOW BITTERNESS.

An expression meaning to harbor resentment, contain anger, and endure suffering.

TO HAVE ONE'S LIVER ON FIRE.

Anger is said to originate from one's liver, so this expression is used when a person is extremely angry.

TO STIR THE FIRE AND BURN ONESELF.

This means to bring trouble upon oneself.

HARSH WORDS AND POOR REASONING
NEVER SETTLE ANYTHING.

DO NOT CREATE IN ANGER WHAT YOU
LACK IN REASON.

MAN IS THE MAIN SOURCE OF HIS
OWN MISERY.

DO NOT UPSET HEAVEN AND EARTH.
An expression to calm someone who is creating a disturbance with loud protest or outbursts of anger.

UNDER HURTFUL ACCUSATIONS
OFTEN LIES A WEAK CASE.
Those who have no defense will use offense.

DON'T JUMP OVER A PIT ONLY TO FALL
INTO A WELL.

BE SLOW TO PROMISE BUT QUICK TO
PERFORM.

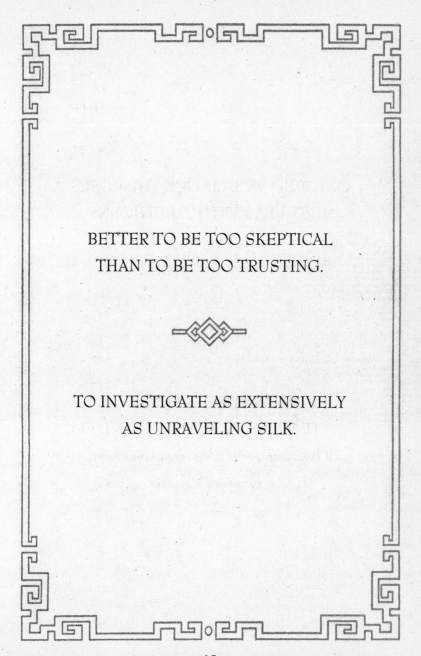

BETTER TO BE TOO SKEPTICAL
THAN TO BE TOO TRUSTING.

TO INVESTIGATE AS EXTENSIVELY
AS UNRAVELING SILK.

ONE WHO WOULD PICK THE ROSES
MUST BEAR WITH THE THORNS.

One learns compromise by accepting
the good with the bad.

COMPROMISE IS ALWAYS A
TEMPORARY ACHIEVEMENT.

When compromise turns into commitment,
it becomes permanent.

ONES WHO ARE UNABLE TO LIVE
UNDER THE SAME SKY.
A common saying to denote bitter enemies
who cannot coexist.

TENACITY AND ADVERSITY
ARE OLD FOES.
Adversity cannot triumph if we remain
tenacious of our goals.

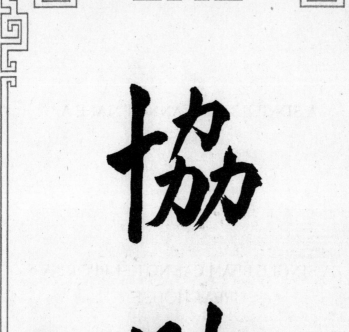

COOPERATION

A SINGLE TREE CANNOT MAKE A
FOREST.

A SINGLE BEAM CANNOT SUPPORT A
GREAT HOUSE.

A BEAUTIFUL FLOWER IS INCOMPLETE
WITHOUT ITS LEAVES.

WHAT IS GOOD FOR THE HIVE IS
GOOD FOR THE BEE.

ONE SINGS, ALL FOLLOW.

An expression that means everyone is in agreement.

A CLOTH IS NOT WOVEN FROM
A SINGLE THREAD.

EACH PERSON EQUALS A GRAIN OF
SAND, BUT A CROWD IS LIKE
A BLOCK OF GOLD.

*Negotiating as a group brings desired
attention and results.*

A BRIDGE IS NOT BUILT FROM ONE
PIECE OF WOOD.

COURTESY

COURTESY IS THE MARK OF A
CIVILIZED PERSON.

FOLLOW THE GOOD AND LEARN
THEIR WAYS.
One is judged by the company one keeps.

DO NOT BE CONCERNED WITH THINGS
OUTSIDE YOUR DOOR.

Mind your own business.

THE COMPANY OF THE WICKED IS LIKE
LIVING IN A FISH MARKET; ONE
BECOMES USED TO THE FOUL ODOR.

*Lack of courtesy is always obvious to others, but not
always to the one who is obnoxious.*

NO SOONER HAS ONE PUSHED ONE
GOURD UNDER WATER THAN
ANOTHER POPS UP.
*Describes being unable to keep up with one crisis
after another.*

ONE WHO DOES NOT BURN INCENSE
WHEN ALL IS WELL BUT CLASPS BUD-
DHA'S FEET WHEN IN TROUBLE.
*An expression used to describe someone who calls on
you only when in trouble.*

ONE WHO HEARS FLATTERY BUT NOT
CRITICISM WILL GO ASTRAY.

FAULTS AND VIRTUES ARE BUT TWO
SIDES OF THE SAME COIN.
Unfair criticism does not distinguish good from bad.

ONE WHO SNORES THE LOUDEST
WILL FALL ASLEEP FIRST.

One who criticizes is oblivious to one's own faults.

ONE WHO BLOWS FUR TO FIND THE
SCAR UNDERNEATH.

*Someone who loves to find fault and will look in the
most unlikely places to uncover flaws.*

BEWARE OF ONE WITH A HONEYED
TONGUE AND A SWORD IN THE BELLY.
A KNOWN ENEMY IS DANGEROUS, BUT
A FALSE FRIEND IS WORSE.

A WEAPON HAS NO LOYALTY BUT TO
THE ONE WHO WIELDS IT.

DON'T BE A TIGER'S HEAD WITH A
SNAKE'S TAIL.

*An incongruous and strange combination used to
describe one who presents an important front with no
substance behind it.*

DO NOT INCREASE THE SIZE OF YOUR
FACE BY BEATING YOUR CHEEKS
SWOLLEN.

*A proverb used to describe those who puff themselves
up trying to impress others.*

IF THE TOP BEAM IS CROOKED ALL
THE REST WILL NOT BE STRAIGHT.

*A saying used to refer to corruption or bribery in
government or large corporations.*

DO NOT BE OUTWARDLY A FIERCE
BULL BUT INWARDLY AS TIMID AS A
MOUSE.

ONE WHO IS AS DISAPPOINTING AS AN
EMPTY DUMPLING.

*This is used for someone who makes empty promises
or fails to live up to expectations.*

DO NOT BE CAUGHT WITH DYE ON
THE FINGERS.

*A warning to those who might be caught stealing or
taking a bribe.*

ONE BECOMES DOUBLE-MINDED
FROM SUSPICION AND GUILT.

Deceptive people find it difficult to believe others.

A PAPER TIGER CANNOT BEAR CLOSE
SCRUTINY.

*This means that the threat is only frightening from a
distance but ineffective when viewed up close.*

DEFEAT IS NEVER A BITTER BREW
UNTIL ONE AGREES TO SWALLOW IT.

Defeat is never final unless we accept it.

TO BE UNHAPPY OVER WHAT ONE
LACKS IS TO WASTE WHAT ONE
ALREADY POSSESSES.

A TINY LEAK WILL EVENTUALLY SINK A MIGHTY SHIP.

A small mistake could have big repercussions.

AN ERROR THE WIDTH OF A HAIR CAN LEAD ONE A THOUSAND MILES ASTRAY.

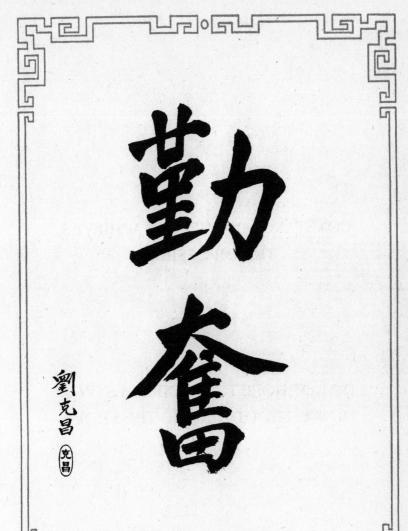

勤奮

DILIGENCE

CONSTANCY OF PURPOSE ACHIEVES
THE IMPOSSIBLE.

DO NOT HOPE TO REACH A DESTINA-
TION WITHOUT LEAVING THE SHORE.

TO CHOP A TREE QUICKLY, SPEND
TWICE THE TIME SHARPENING
YOUR AX.

A MAN OF LEISURE WILL NEVER TASTE
THE FRUIT OF SUCCESS.

THINK BEFORE YOU SPEAK BUT DO
NOT SPEAK ALL THAT YOU THINK.

MASTERING DISCRETION IS GREATER
THAN EMPLOYING ELOQUENCE.

*Knowing when to speak is more important than
being an eloquent speaker.*

A FOOL'S HEART IS FOUND IN HIS
MOUTH.

THOSE WHO SPEND ALL THEIR TIME
TALKING WILL HAVE NO TIME TO
THINK.

FOR THE LOVE OF MONEY, TRUTH
WILL FALL SILENT.
Silence can be bought.

SILENCE CONDEMNS MORE EFFEC-
TIVELY THAN LOUD ACCUSATIONS.

IF THE ARM IS BROKEN, HIDE IT IN
THE SLEEVE.

*A popular saying that means one should not display
one's dirty linen in public.*

A RICH MAN MUST FEAR PUBLICITY AS
A PIG SHOULD FEAR BEING FAT.

*The more one has to lose, the more discreet one
should be.*

EVEN THE POWERFUL OX HAS NO
DEFENSE AGAINST FLIES.
Rumors and lies can plague even the most powerful.

AN IDLE STORY CAN QUICKLY BECOME
FACT IN THE MOUTHS OF HUNDREDS.

GOOD DEEDS NEVER LEAVE HOME,
BAD ONES ECHO A THOUSAND MILES.

TRUE WORDS MAY NOT BE PLEASANT,
PLEASANT WORDS MAY NOT BE TRUE.

WHAT YOU SEE IS REAL; WHAT YOU
HEAR MAY NOT BE.

DO NOT JUDGE MATTERS FROM A
SINGLE OCCURRENCE.

TWO HANDS SHOULD BE TWICE AS
BUSY AS ONE TONGUE.

TO HEAR FOOTSTEPS BUT FIND NO
ONE APPROACHING. . . .
*A saying that pokes fun at someone who makes
many promises but cannot deliver.*

ONLY SHOVEL THE SNOW FROM YOUR
OWN DOORSTEP.
*Do not mind other people's business since you can-
not be in their position.*

DO NOT LAY A CORPSE AT SOMEONE ELSE'S DOOR.

This means do not involve others in trouble that does not concern them.

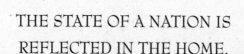

THE STATE OF A NATION IS
REFLECTED IN THE HOME.

ONCE ONE IS A TEACHER ONE
BECOMES A PARENT FOR LIFE.
*The Chinese believe the responsibility of a teacher is
the same as that of a parent.*

WHEREVER ONE FINDS COMFORT CAN
BE CALLED HOME.

THE LAMB KNEELS TO SUCKLE.
A favorite expression describing filial piety, gratitude,
and respect for one's parents.

A PEARL FROM AN OLD OYSTER.
A Chinese saying about a precious offspring born to
someone who is almost past childbearing age.

WHAT IS FATED TO BE YOURS WILL
ALWAYS RETURN TO YOU.

OFTEN ONE FINDS DESTINY JUST
WHERE ONE HIDES TO AVOID IT.

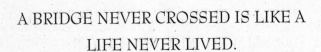

A BRIDGE NEVER CROSSED IS LIKE A
LIFE NEVER LIVED.

FATE LEADS THOSE WHO ARE WILLING
BUT MUST PUSH THOSE WHO ARE
NOT.

A GREAT FIRE MAY FOLLOW A TINY
SPARK.

SET FIRE TO THE FOREST TO DRIVE
OUT THE WOLVES.

*A saying used to describe drastic measures that are
not practical.*

劉克昌
[克昌]

FORESIGHT

WEAVING A NET IS BETTER THAN
PRAYING FOR FISH AT THE EDGE OF
THE WATER.

BEND ONE CUBIT, MAKE EIGHT CUBITS
STRAIGHT.

*Correcting a problem in the beginning prevents more
problems down the road.*

DO NOT BUILD UPON THE SAND WHAT
IS PERMANENT.

*Be sure to have a good, firm foundation before
investing time, effort, and money in any endeavor.*

FIRST RESOLVE WHAT MUST BE DONE;
SOLUTIONS WILL THEN BECOME
EVIDENT.

ONE MUST CUT BEFORE FILING,
CARVE BEFORE POLISHING.

REMEMBER TO DIG THE WELL LONG
BEFORE YOU GET THIRSTY.

FORTUNE

WHAT FIRST APPEARS AS A CALAMITY
MAY LATER BRING GOOD FORTUNE.

THE TIDE MUST REACH ITS LOWEST
BEFORE IT TURNS.

LOOK TO YOUR ENEMY FOR A CHANCE
TO SUCCEED.

FORTUNE COMES IN MANY DISGUISES.

NO ONE WILL STAY ATOP THE WHEEL
OF FORTUNE ALL THE TIME.

EARTH IS TO THE DEAD WHAT GOLD IS
TO THE LIVING.
*The living and the dead have different needs. A
reversal of fortune.*

FORTUNE HAS A FICKLE HEART AND A
SHORT MEMORY.

BE AS FORTUNATE AS ONE WHO
RESTS ON HIGH PILLOWS.

*A saying that denotes someone who lives an elevated
life of ease and luxury without any worries.*

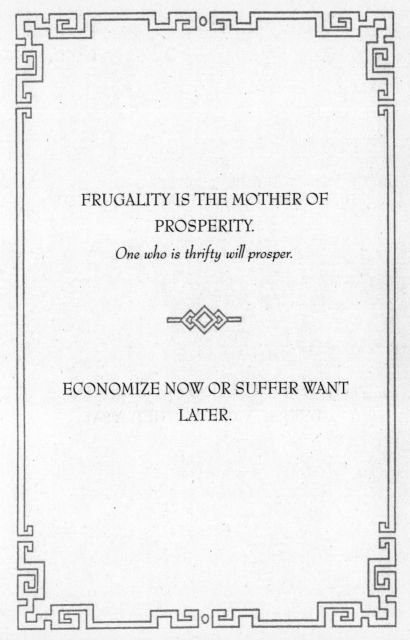

FRUGALITY IS THE MOTHER OF
PROSPERITY.

One who is thrifty will prosper.

ECONOMIZE NOW OR SUFFER WANT
LATER.

BE FRUGAL IN PROSPERITY, FEAR NOT
IN ADVERSITY.

Store and save for that rainy day.

PROSPERITY BRINGS US FRIENDS,
ADVERSITY DRIVES THEM AWAY.

DO NOT DRAW A SNAKE AND ADD FEET
TO IT.

*Overenthusiasm causes unnecessary work. Often
used to describe someone who is overdoing things.*

WHEN THE ITCH IS INSIDE THE BOOT,
SCRATCHING OUTSIDE PROVIDES
LITTLE CONSOLATION.

*Expresses the futility of not being able to deal directly
with a problem.*

TO SEE ANOTHER'S DUST BUT BE
UNABLE TO OVERTAKE HIM.

A BUDDHA MADE OF MUD CROSSING
A RIVER CANNOT PROTECT EVEN
HIMSELF.

*The buddha symbolizes one who is powerful, but in
this vulnerable situation he is not even able to take
care of himself. Therefore, it is pointless to expect the
buddha to assist us under such conditions.*

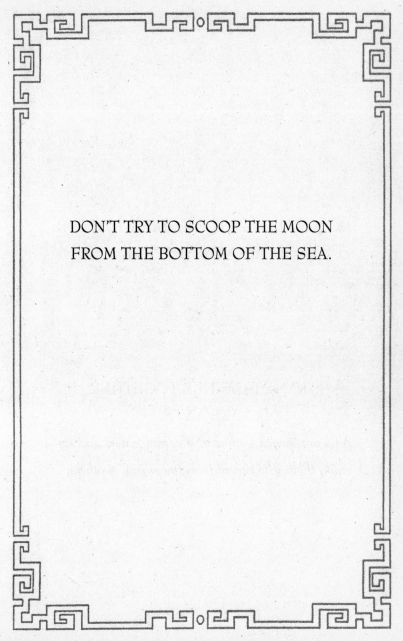

DON'T TRY TO SCOOP THE MOON
FROM THE BOTTOM OF THE SEA.

DO NOT LEARN TO DESIRE WHAT ONE
DOES NOT DESERVE.

DO NOT GATHER TOGETHER
LIKE ANTS.

Ants are likened to thieves or carrion eaters and signify those who benefit from the misery of others.

DO NOT HAVE EYES THAT ARE BIGGER
THAN YOUR STOMACH.

*Common Chinese saying from parents to children
who take more food than they can eat.*

OUR NEEDS ARE FEW BUT OUR WANTS
INCREASE WITH OUR POSSESSIONS.

Greed feeds upon itself.

GREED COMES INTO ONE'S HEART TO
STEAL PEACE OF MIND.

THERE IS NO GREATER CALAMITY
THAN BEING CONSUMED BY GREED.

LUST AND GREED HAVE NO LIMIT.

FAT FRIES AND BURNS ITSELF.

*This saying is used to describe greedy or powerful
people who are usually the instruments of their own
destruction.*

HAPPINESS

A HAPPY PERSON IS ONE NOT
TRAPPED BY FAME AND FORTUNE.

IT IS WEALTH ENOUGH TO LEARN THE
MEANING OF CONTENTMENT.

Happy hearts are rich in so many ways.

SOLITUDE IS ENJOYED ONLY WHEN
ONE IS AT PEACE WITH ONESELF.
*One who has a guilty conscience finds it difficult to
live with oneself or to enjoy one's own company.*

WHEN YOU DRINK OF THE SPRING BE
THANKFUL FOR THE SOURCE.
*Know where your blessings come from and give
thanks. Do not pollute the source if you have to drink
the water.*

THOSE WHO SEEK HARMONY KNOW
HOW TO FIND IT.

SATISFIED PEOPLE DO
NOT COMPLAIN.

WATER THAT HAS REACHED ITS LEVEL
DOES NOT FLOW.

Sayings that describe how one should treat others.

One must recognize the limits of endurance.

Resentment or discontentment is seen as water over-

flowing. If water is contained to its level, there will be

no complaints.

COUNT NOT WHAT IS LOST BUT WHAT
IS LEFT.

SORROWING HEARTS ARE ALWAYS
UNSETTLED.

FORGIVENESS IS AN ACT OF THE
HEART.

Forgiveness *is written in Chinese with the word for act* *or compliance above the symbol for the heart* 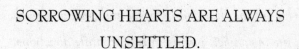 .

PUT YOUR HEART AT REST.

This means to stop worrying.

WISHES OF MIND AND HEART ARE AS
HARD TO CONTROL AS A HORSE AND
AN APE.

*This means that one's mental and emotional wishes
are in conflict, pulling in two separate directions.*

A CALM HEART ADJUSTS TO MANY
CHANGES.

TO ACCOMMODATE ALL THINGS,
ENLARGE YOUR HEART.

A generous heart knows no bounds.

MUSIC CHEERS THE HEART AND
WARMS THE DISPOSITION.

A KIND PERSON'S MOUTH IS FOUND
IN THE HEART.
*A compassionate person will speak through thought-
ful acts rather than just saying the right things to
impress others.*

GOOD HEART, GOOD REWARD.
A just heart has its own reward.

WE CAN FIND NO WEALTH ABOVE A
HEALTHY BODY AND A HAPPY HEART.

USE WITH A SMALL HEART.
*Means to use something with caution or to handle
something fragile with extreme care.*

THE WORST PRISON IS ONE MADE OF
THE HEART.
*One who cannot or will not permit oneself to love or
forgive is one's own jailer.*

HONOR

A NOBLE ANCESTRY CANNOT GUARAN-
TEE A NOBLE CHARACTER.

WHEN A LEOPARD DIES, HE LEAVES
HIS COAT.
WHEN A MAN DIES, HE LEAVES HIS
NAME.

AN HONORABLE PERSON IS A
MAJORITY OF ONE.

A CLEAR CONSCIENCE IS THE
GREATEST ARMOR.
One who is faultless can withstand criticism and
adversity.

VIRTUE TRAVELS UPHILL, VICE
TRAVELS DOWNHILL.

LIFE AND SHAME ARE NEVER EQUAL
TO DEATH AND GLORY.

CHANGE THE SKIN, WASH THE HEART.
This means to reform one's character completely.

TO SCRAPE THE LIGHT OFF
ONE'S FACE.
To suddenly lose one's reputation or credibility.

A MAN MUST DESPISE HIMSELF
BEFORE OTHERS WILL.

HATE RISES LIKE SMOKE AROUND ONE
WHO SURPASSES ONE'S PEERS.
Envy and anger among those who once considered us
their equals are natural outcomes when we receive
success, fame, or good fortune.

BE ON A HORSE WHEN YOU GO IN
SEARCH OF A BETTER ONE.

A Chinese admonition that one should preferably have a job when one goes in search of a better one. Another example is to drive a nice car when you go to purchase another so that you will not be at the mercy of others or be taken advantage of.

HE WANTS TO BUY THE BEST HORSE:
ONE THAT DOES NOT EAT GRASS.

This proverb describes a person who is too calculating, unrealistic, and never satisfied. This person wants something for nothing or wishes for something that does not exist, like a horse that does not eat grass.

A CLEVER HORSE NEEDS ONLY ONE TOUCH OF THE WHIP.

Someone who is intelligent and astute needs only one little hint to understand the situation.

REIN IN THE HORSE AT THE EDGE OF THE CLIFF.

To pull oneself back at the last moment and stop before plunging over the precipice.

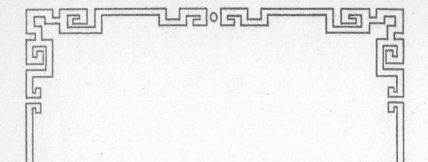

THE OLD HORSE WILL KNOW THE WAY.

DON'T DOCTOR A DEAD HORSE AS IF
IT WERE ALIVE.

LARGE DEMANDS ON ONESELF AND LITTLE DEMANDS ON OTHERS KEEP RESENTMENT AT BAY.

IT'S SOMETHING NOT WORTH HANGING ON THE TEETH.

A polite response when someone thanks you for a big favor. This proverb uses exaggeration to minimize the importance of the service by saying that it was so inconsequential that it could not even hang between the teeth.

INDECISIVENESS BREEDS
CONFUSION.

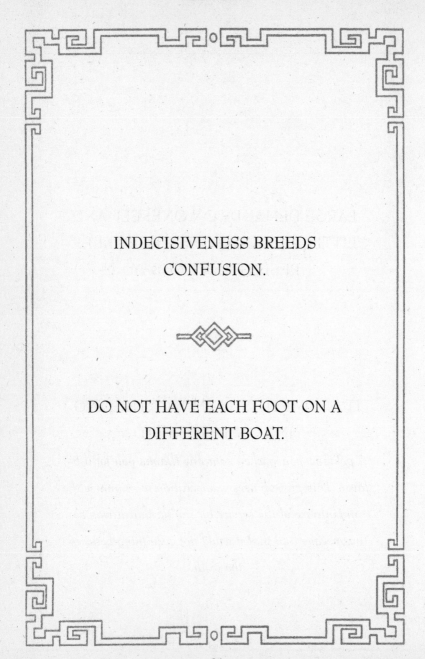

DO NOT HAVE EACH FOOT ON A
DIFFERENT BOAT.

RETICENCE BUILDS A FORTRESS IN
THE MIND.

One who is unsure or fearful puts up mental barriers.

TO DRAW THE BOW BUT NOT RELEASE
THE ARROW.

*To make threats without following through with
positive action.*

INSPIRATION

COWARDS HAVE DREAMS, BRAVE MEN
HAVE VISIONS.

ONE'S MERITS SHOULD NOT BE A HIN-
DRANCE TO ONE'S PROGRESS.

REVIEW PAST LESSONS TO DISCOVER
ANEW.

LEARNING IS LIKE THE HORIZON:
THERE IS NO LIMIT.

WITHOUT EXPERIENCE WE WILL NOT
GAIN FULL KNOWLEDGE.

TO FEEL THE CATCH OF THE LOCK.
*Used to describe one who is able to comprehend the
key to the situation, the crux of the matter, or the
most important point in a discussion.*

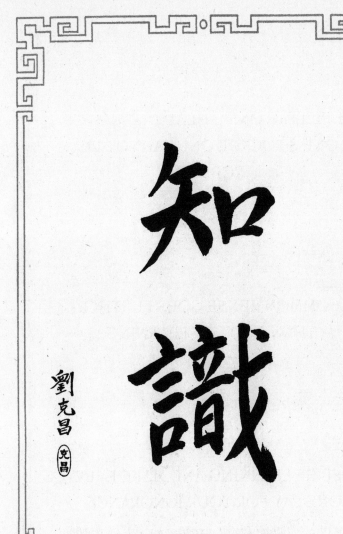

知識

劉克昌

KNOWLEDGE

BY FILLING ONE'S HEAD INSTEAD OF ONE'S POCKET, ONE CANNOT BE ROBBED.

COMMON SENSE GOES FURTHER THAN A LOT OF LEARNING.

DESPISE LEARNING AND MAKE EVERY-ONE PAY FOR YOUR IGNORANCE.

Ignorance (illiteracy) is an expense society as a whole must bear.

ONE WHO DOES NOT LIKE TO READ IS
EQUAL TO ONE WHO CANNOT READ.

A NIGHT WITHOUT MOON OR STARS IS
LIKE AN IGNORANT MIND.

WEED THROUGH THE OLD TO BRING
FORTH THE NEW.

A saying attributed to Chairman Mao regarding the
people's revolution against old ideas and tradition.

WHEAT STALKS HEAVY WITH GRAIN
LEARN HOW TO BOW THEIR HEADS.
*Matured stalks symbolize learned and humble per-
sons who acknowledge that they do not know every-
thing, while empty-headed young stalks without fruit
stand upright in their arrogance and ignorance.*

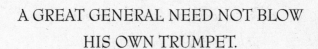

A GREAT GENERAL NEED NOT BLOW
HIS OWN TRUMPET.

ONE WHO IS FIT TO SIT FACING THE
SOUTH.

*Only a ruler or leader was considered worthy enough
to sit facing south, as this was the most favorable
direction.*

ONE LOOKS UP AT A WORTHY PERSON
AS ONE LOOKS UP TO A MOUNTAIN.

IF THERE IS A STRONG GENERAL
THERE WILL BE NO WEAK SOLDIERS.

*A good leader will know how to assess, train, and
utilize people to their full potential.*

PULL A STRAND OF SILK FROM A
TANGLED MASS.

To restore order to disorder.

ONE WHO IS WISE IN STRATEGY
CARRIES AN ARMY IN ONE'S MIND.

*A person who knows how to plan skillfully and to
improvise is as powerful as an army.*

WITHOUT THE FIRE OF ENTHUSIASM
THERE IS NO WARMTH IN VICTORY.

IT DOES NOT MATTER IF THE CAT IS
BLACK OR WHITE, SO LONG AS IT
CATCHES MICE.

*This saying was attributed to Deng Xiaoping who
used it to respond to criticism as an example that the
end will justify the means.*

生活

LIVELIHOOD

DO NOT BECOME A MONK OR A NUN SO LATE IN LIFE.

A proverb that dissuades people from changing their professions or doing things they have not been trained for.

DO NOT BE A FROG SITTING AT THE BOTTOM OF A WELL.

A frog at the bottom of a well has no prospects and is in a very difficult position unless it can leap out. It only sees a small patch of sky, so its view of the world is limited.

TO BE AS UNCOMFORTABLE AS
SITTING ON A RUG OF NEEDLES.
To be in a difficult, unrewarding job.

HAVING TO WATCH THE EYEBROWS
AND COUNTENANCE OF ANOTHER.
*This means that one is in a servile position and must
wait upon another or be at the mercy of a superior's
disposition.*

ONE WHO MAY BE EASY TO SERVE YET DIFFICULT TO PLEASE.

This describes one who is always unhappy but never forthright about one's feelings, and one who is difficult to work for.

EXIT THE DOOR, CHECK THE WEATHER; ENTER THE DOOR, CHECK THE FACE.

This is an old saying that states that before one leaves home, one will look outside to check the weather. But when one returns home, one must look inside at the occupant's face to see if he or she is in a happy or unhappy mood.

BETTER TO LEARN ONE THING WELL
THAN TO KNOW TEN SUPERFICIALLY.

A MAN MUST DEPEND ON HIS ENVI-
RONMENT.

One who lives by the water must learn to fish, while
one who lives on fertile land must learn to plant
crops.

LONGEVITY

MAY YOU LIVE AS LONG AS THE
SOUTHERN MOUNTAIN AND ENJOY
HAPPINESS AS BOUNTIFUL AS THE
EASTERN SEA.

*The traditional Chinese wish for longevity is always
combined with happiness because a long life without
happiness is a burden and a curse.*

THE LEAVES OF A TREE ARE MANY,
BUT THE ROOT IS ONE.

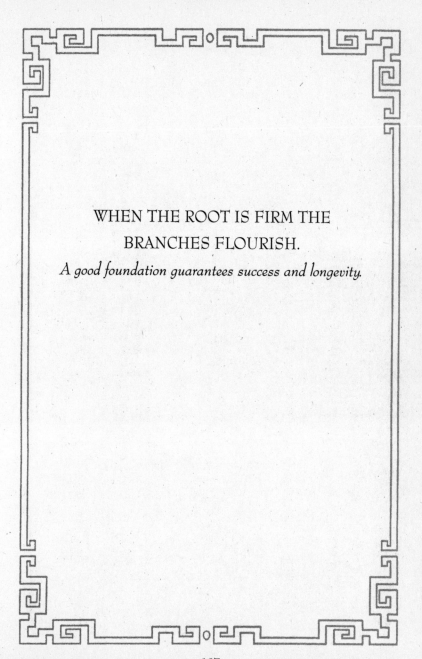

WHEN THE ROOT IS FIRM THE
BRANCHES FLOURISH.

A good foundation guarantees success and longevity.

LOVE

LOVE AS RARE AS TWIN LOTUS ON A
SINGLE STALK.
*A symbolic Chinese analogy of a happy and devoted
couple.*

A COUPLE WHO SPEND ONE HAPPY
DAY TOGETHER ARE BLESSED WITH A
HUNDRED DAYS OF AFFECTION.
*An old saying that describes conjugal
harmony and bliss.*

SEEKING AFFECTION AS A SUN-
FLOWER FACES THE SUN.

LOVE FOR A PERSON MUST EXTEND
TO THE CROWS ON HIS ROOF.
One's love for others must include acceptance of their
imperfections.

ONE WHO MINDS THE FEELINGS OF
OTHERS IS NO FOOL.

THE TILES ARE BROKEN AND THE ICE IS MELTED.

A saying denoting that fame is dead and the glory is gone.

TO BE BORN UNDER THE POST-HORSE'S STAR.

This refers to someone who is always having to travel or who is as busy as the post-horse making daily deliveries. One who is fated never to stay long in one place.

BLESSINGS COME BUT ONE AT A TIME,
MISFORTUNE VISITS IN MULTIPLES.

*A saying lamenting the fact that bad luck often
comes in threes.*

TO SIT ON A COLD BENCH; TO HAVE A
COLD STOVE.

*To be in a job or position with no prospects, or to be
in a dead end.*

ONE DOES NOT DRINK POISON TO
QUENCH A THIRST.

*To be self-destructive and impractical. Jumping from
the frying pan into the fire.*

MISFORTUNE CONQUERS TIMID SOULS WHILE GREAT MINDS SUBDUE MISFORTUNE.

THE POOR ARE THOSE WITHOUT TALENTS; THE WEAK ARE THOSE WITHOUT ASPIRATIONS.

TO LIVE LONG AND WELL, EMPLOY
MODERATION.

IF ONE EATS LESS,
ONE WILL TASTE MORE.

TO EXTEND YOUR LIFE BY A YEAR,
TAKE ONE LESS BITE EACH MEAL.

MORALITY

ONE WHO IS A SLAVE TO ONE'S
SENSES CANNOT REIN ONE'S WILL
INTO SUBMISSION.

SENDING CHARCOAL IN THE SNOW IS
BETTER THAN ADDING FLOWERS TO A
BROCADE.

*This saying means that friends who flatter us when
we are doing well are "adding flowers" to an already
intricate and richly decorated fabric, while true
friends will bring "charcoal in the snow," or give us
assistance in our hour of need.*

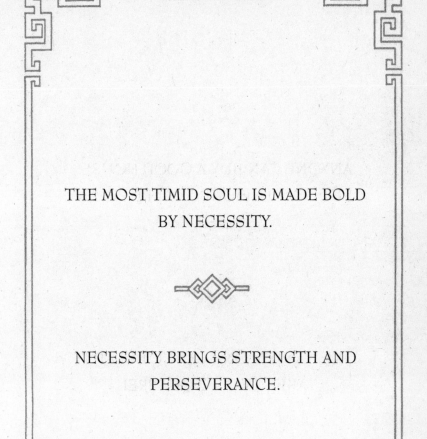

THE MOST TIMID SOUL IS MADE BOLD
BY NECESSITY.

NECESSITY BRINGS STRENGTH AND
PERSEVERANCE.

ANYONE CAN BUY A GOOD HOUSE, BUT GOOD NEIGHBORS ARE PRICE-LESS.

ONE HAND ALONE CANNOT CLAP, IT TAKES TWO TO QUARREL.

YOUR TEN FINGERS WILL ALWAYS CURL INWARD.

A common reference to nepotism. It is as natural as one's fingers bending toward the palm.

THEY ARE ALL BADGERS FROM THE SAME MOUND.

A group of people who all think and even look alike. Everyone assumes a single identity.

WHEN A CENTIPEDE DIES ON THE WALL IT DOES NOT FALL DOWN.

This refers to laws that are no longer useful, old institutions that have outlived their need, or bureaucratic people who cling to power.

DO NOT LOOK AT OTHERS WITH THE EYES OF A DOG.

A dog values only its master and looks down on everyone else as being unequal to its master. This saying means that one should not make judgments in such a foolish way.

IVY MUST CLING TO THE WALL; POR-
RIDGE WILL STICK TO THE POT.
*It is difficult to change the nature of things. Old
habits die hard.*

WINNING AN ARGUMENT DOES NOT
MEAN ONE HAS CONVINCED ONE'S
OPPONENT.
*Changing another's mind is more difficult than being
able to debate and argue skillfully.*

OPPORTUNITY

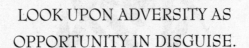

LOOK UPON ADVERSITY AS
OPPORTUNITY IN DISGUISE.

CRISIS BRINGS OPPORTUNITY AND
CHANGE.

*In Chinese, "crisis" is composed of two words. The
first means "danger" and the second means "opportunity," "motion," and "change."*

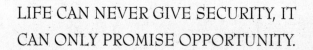

LIFE CAN NEVER GIVE SECURITY, IT
CAN ONLY PROMISE OPPORTUNITY.

ADDING FROST TO SNOW.
To be faced with one problem after another, crisis
upon crisis.

PATIENCE

PATIENCE IS A TREE WITH BITTER
ROOTS THAT BEARS SWEET FRUITS.

DO NOT PULL THE SEEDLINGS TO
HELP THEM GROW FASTER.
*Another admonition is: "Hair does not grow faster
by being pulled." This advises against unnecessary
meddling or overenthusiasm.*

PATIENCE IS WISDOM IN WAITING.

ORDER MOVES SLOWLY BUT SURELY;
DISORDER, ALWAYS IN A HURRY.

INSPIRATION COMES FROM
PERSPIRATION.

A BIRD CANNOT FLY UNTIL ITS
FEATHERS ARE FULL-GROWN.

Do not attempt to do something until you are ready.

A SUPERIOR MAN ACTS WITH JUSTICE.

THE SEASONS WILL RETURN; ALL
THINGS ARE RENEWED.
The difficulties will pass and all will be well again.

PEACE ONLY COMES WHEN
REASON RULES.

LAWS ARE USELESS WHEN MEN ARE
PURE, UNENFORCEABLE WHEN MEN
ARE CORRUPT.

MAY A HAPPY STAR ALWAYS LIGHT
YOUR PATH.

MAY IT ALWAYS BE SPRING WITH YOU.
In China, spring is a time of joy and celebration.

PERSEVERANCE

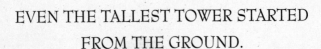

EVEN THE TALLEST TOWER STARTED
FROM THE GROUND.
All things can be accomplished one step at a time.

GEMS ARE POLISHED BY RUBBING,
JUST AS MEN ARE MADE BRILLIANT BY
TRIALS.

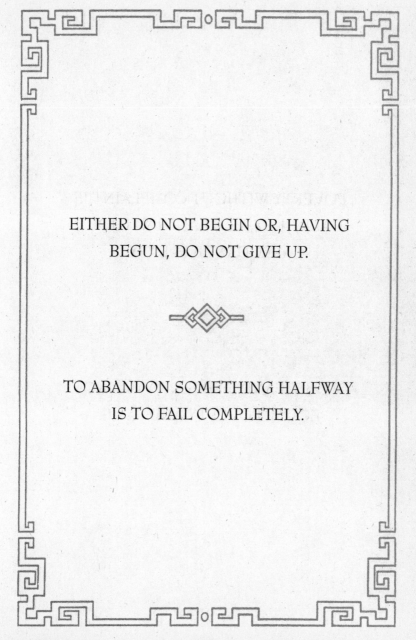

EITHER DO NOT BEGIN OR, HAVING
BEGUN, DO NOT GIVE UP.

TO ABANDON SOMETHING HALFWAY
IS TO FAIL COMPLETELY.

POVERTY WITHOUT COMPLAINT IS
HARD, JUST AS WEALTH WITHOUT
ARROGANCE IS EASY.

WEALTH AND OBSCURITY CANNOT
EQUAL POVERTY AND FAME.

BURN ONE DAY'S GATHERING OF FIRE-
WOOD ON THE SAME DAY.

This means to live from hand to mouth and not have
anything left over, to barely get by from day to day.

FAVORS ARE ONLY REMEMBERED
WHILE A MAN LIVES.

All the good one does is often forgotten when one
dies. Dead men cannot repay favors.

IF THE WIND BLOWS FROM ONE DIRECTION, SO WILL A TREE GROW INCLINED.

A twisted or bent tree is a symbol of prejudice or bigotry because it only receives wind from one side, just like a person who subscribes to a single point of view and is unable to understand the position of others.

DO NOT HAVE YOUR EYES GROWING ON YOUR FOREHEAD.

Used to refer to people who are proud and often pretend not to see others. Eyes do not belong on the forehead, and people would look foolish and vain if they acted as if they did.

DO NOT BE AN EARTHEN POT TRYING TO SOUND LIKE THUNDER.

This describes someone who is mediocre trying to make a lot of noise to impress others.

A CLAP OF THUNDER RESOUNDS
ALL OVER.

*To make a stunning announcement or cause a
great change or controversy.*

ONE'S SHADOW GROWS LARGER THAN
LIFE WHEN ADMIRED BY THE LIGHT
OF THE MOON.

*A proverb that makes fun of a person who has an
inflated image of himself or herself.*

利潤

PROFIT

TO LOSE A SHEEP BUT GAIN AN OX.

To lose something of lesser value and gain something

of greater value as a result.

TO LOSE A HALBERD BUT GAIN A

LANCE.

To lose and gain something of equal value.

FAILURE IS THE MOTHER OF SUCCESS.

GREAT EVENTS MAY COME FROM
HUMBLE CIRCUMSTANCES.

IF THERE ARE NO CLOUDS THERE
WILL BE NO RAIN.

*Success cannot come from nowhere. There must be
efforts made to produce results.*

FOOD AND FODDER MUST PRECEDE TROOPS AND HORSES.

Do things in the proper order. The equivalent of the saying that the horse must go before the cart.

ONE GUEST DOES NOT TROUBLE TWO HOSTS.

This means that one should not ask two people to do the same task. Allow one person to assume sole responsibility or none at all.

SINCERITY

TO TELL ONLY HALF THE TRUTH IS TO
GIVE LIFE TO A NEW LIE.

THE LONGER THE EXPLANATION THE
BIGGER THE LIE.

ELOQUENCE PROVIDES ONLY PERSUA-
SION, BUT TRUTH BUYS LOYALTY.

TRUTH IS OFTEN DISGUISED AS JEST.

THE ONE WHO PLANTS THE TREE IS
NOT THE ONE WHO WILL ENJOY ITS
SHADE.

*This refers to those who do things for the benefit of
others, knowing they will not reap any reward for
their kindness.*

STRATEGY

IN WAR THERE CAN NEVER BE TOO
MUCH DECEPTION.

BEAT THE GRASS TO FRIGHTEN THE
SNAKES.

*To flush out the enemy or to disturb those one does
not like in hopes of driving them away.*

DO NOT MAKE A RULE ONLY TO FALL
FOUL OF IT.

This means to become trapped by one's own device.

SIT ATOP THE MOUNTAIN AND WATCH THE TIGERS FIGHT.

This saying refers to one who watches two opponents contend with each other, hoping that both will be eliminated.

TO GATHER AN AUDIENCE, START A FIGHT.

A way to get attention or create a diversion.

TO CONQUER ONE HUNDRED TIMES OUT OF ONE HUNDRED, STUDY YOUR OPPONENT WELL.

The Chinese believe the key to victory is to know your opponent as well as you know yourself.

DO NOT HIT THE FLY THAT LANDS ON THE TIGER'S HEAD.

Warns against having good intentions
but bad timing.

WHENEVER THE WATER RISES, THE BOAT WILL RISE, TOO.

This proverb is commonly used in politics. It
describes someone who associates with people in
power in order to rise with them by being in the right
place with the right party. To be carried on another's
coattails.

IF THERE IS A WAVE THERE
MUST BE A WIND.
This means to understand the
consequences of one's actions.

THREE SIMPLE SHOEMAKERS EQUAL
ONE BRILLIANT STRATEGIST.
—ZHU GELIANG
A famous saying comparing the combined intelligence
of three ordinary people, such as shoemakers, to that
of one of the greatest Chinese generals and strate-
gists. This means unity equals strength.

WAIT LONG, STRIKE FAST.

A strategy that advocates great patience combined with quick decisiveness.

BE IN READINESS FOR FAVORABLE WINDS.

Actually, the Chinese translation is: Be in readiness for the east wind! This is taken from an important battle in the war classic Romance of the Three Kingdoms. *A general had only one chance to storm a fortress and, at a determined time, all of his ships had to depend on the east wind to make the surprise attack successful.*

USE EVERY STEP AS YOUR BASE.

*Depend only on yourself. Do not rely on the
support of others.*

IF ONE MAN GUARDS A NARROW PASS, TEN THOUSAND CANNOT GET THROUGH.

*A strategically placed barrier can
achieve the impossible.*

AN OVERTURNED CART AHEAD WARNS THE ONE BEHIND.

*Learn from the experiences of others and observe
before proceeding on new ventures.*

DO NOT LIFT A ROCK ONLY TO DROP
IT ON YOUR OWN FOOT.

Do not make changes just for the sake of change.

Things could get worse.

DO NOT REMAIN IN THE OPEN WHEN
THE ENEMY IS CONCEALED.

OF THE THIRTY-SIX STRATEGEMS, "RUNNING AWAY" IS THE BEST ONE.

The Thirty-six Chinese Strategems is a renowned treatise on the art of war. It is often said that the last one, which recommends running away, is probably the wisest of them all.

WHEN ONE IS PREPARED, DIFFICULTIES DO NOT COME.

It is a common perception that when one is ready for all contingencies, they seldom arise.

MONKEYS MUST DISPERSE ONCE THEIR TREE FALLS.

To get rid of a group of people, remove their common bond or leader and they will disperse.

TO FORCE THE UNTRAINED INTO BATTLE IS TO THROW THEM AWAY.

A Confucian saying that advises against wasting one's resources.

KILL THE CHICKEN TO FRIGHTEN THE MONKEY.

To sacrifice or punish the less important as an example to the real culprit.

THE BEST TACTICIANS ARE NEVER
IMPULSIVE; THE BEST LEADERS ARE
NEVER ARROGANT.

SPECTATORS OFTEN HAVE A BETTER
VIEW THAN THE PROTAGONISTS.
*People who are too close to their problems may not
see the whole picture as impartial observers do.*

DO NOT ATTEMPT TO FIX
WITH A SINGLE BITE.
*A usual retort to someone who gives a simplistic solu-
tion to a complex problem without understanding all
the implications.*

SUCCESS

FAILURE IS NOT FALLING DOWN BUT
REFUSING TO GET UP.

INGENUITY LIGHTS THE
PATH TO SUCCESS.

SUSPICION WILL CHASE THE WIND
AND CLUTCH AT SHADOWS.

TO THE FEARFUL, THE REFLECTION
OF A BOW IS THAT OF A SNAKE.

This means that, when one is frightened and over-imaginative, one sees the reflection of an enemy or something sinister in innocent things.

優勢

SUPERIORITY

IT TAKES A TREE TEN YEARS TO
MATURE; IT TAKES A MAN ONE HUN-
DRED YEARS TO FORM.

Maturity and wisdom take a lifetime to achieve.

THE MIGHTY TREE MUST
CATCH THE WIND.

*The tree in this proverb refers to rich or famous per-
sons who suffer controversy, lawsuits, and unwanted
publicity because of their high profile.*

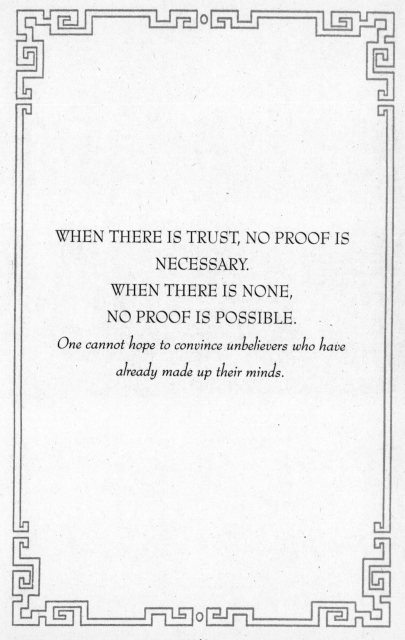

WHEN THERE IS TRUST, NO PROOF IS
NECESSARY.
WHEN THERE IS NONE,
NO PROOF IS POSSIBLE.
*One cannot hope to convince unbelievers who have
already made up their minds.*

VICTORY

OCCUPY THE HIGHER GROUND TO
EXERCISE CONTROL.
*To gain the upper hand and take control
of a situation.*

FIGHT ONLY WHEN YOU CAN WIN;
MOVE AWAY WHEN YOU CANNOT.

財富

WEALTH

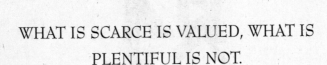

WHAT IS SCARCE IS VALUED, WHAT IS
PLENTIFUL IS NOT.

ONE COURTS MISFORTUNE BY
FLAUNTING WEALTH.

智慧

WISDOM

IN A CRISIS PEOPLE GROW WISDOM.

INTELLIGENCE IS ENDOWED, BUT
WISDOM IS LEARNED.

WISDOM IS ATTAINED BY LEARNING
WHEN TO HOLD ONE'S TONGUE.

DO NOT GAZE AT THE SKY FROM THE
BOTTOM OF A WELL.
*A saying that dissuades one from having a very lim-
ited view of one's possibilities.*

WISE MEN MAY NOT BE LEARNED,
LEARNED MEN MAY NOT BE WISE.

ONE WHO SECURES THE GOOD OF
OTHERS HAS SECURED ONE'S OWN.

GRAIN IS THE TREASURE OF
ALL TREASURES.

IT IS ALWAYS EASIER FOR ONE MAN
TO SOLVE ANOTHER MAN'S PROBLEM.

THE WISE MAN IS ALWAYS GOOD, BUT
A GOOD MAN IS NOT ALWAYS WISE.

DO NOT JUDGE A PERSON UNTIL THE
LID OF HIS COFFIN IS CLOSED.

*One's story is not finished until one dies. There is
always hope for someone to reform or repent at the
last moment.*

IT TAKES TRUE HEROISM TO CON-
QUER ONESELF.

One's battle with oneself is hardest to win.

WORRY NEVER THWARTED DESTINY.

No one ever influenced or changed fate by worrying.

THE BODY'S PAIN CAN BE
CONTROLLED, BUT THAT OF
THE MIND CANNOT.

Mental or emotional pain is above the physical realm,
but can cause people extreme distress.